DROPS OF AWESOME

To my Young Women, who remind me that I'm
not the only one putting Drops in my Bucket.

Published by Familius LLC, www.familius.com

Familius books are available at special discounts for bulk purchases for sales promotions, family
or corporate use. Special editions, including personalized covers, excerpts of existing books,
or books with corporate logos, can be created in large quantities for special needs. For more
information, contact Premium Sales at 559-876-2170 or email specialmarkets@familius.com.

Library of Congress Catalog-in-Publication Data
2014944990
pISBN 978-1939629272

Printed in the United States of America

Edited by Aimee Hancock
Cover and book design by David Miles

10 9 8 7 6 5 4 3 2 1
First Edition

Kathryn Thompson

DROPS OF AWESOME

THE-YOU'RE-MORE-AWESOME-THAN-YOU-THINK

JOURNAL

FAMILIUS

PREFACE

for years I've been writing about my life and posting my thoughts online. I suppose you could call me a journaling exhibitionist. Where a normal person writes a journal, I write a journal and then try to get as many people to read it as possible.

This started as a hobby—a medically mandated hobby. When my brain lost its way after the birth of my second child, the doctor said, "Do something creative." Since my kids were too little to carry a boom mic, I decided not to pursue my passion for filmmaking, and instead, I took to the interwebs, weaving stories out of the everyday occurrences in the lives of my then family of four.

I wrote, and sometimes people read. Sometimes people paid me to write. Every once in a while blogging meant cool experiences, like getting to speak on panels at conferences around the country, meeting the CEO of a fabulous charitable foundation, or spending the day with a crew from the *Today Show* following me around to film a segment.

Most of the time it meant getting real about my emotions and hoping to connect with other people who could relate to my experiences. (*You love marshmallows too?! I am not alone in this big wide digital universe!*) Usually I was a smart aleck, trying to find humor in the everyday. I got stuck in a snowstorm with my rental car return guy for several awkward hours and nearly starved to death? At least I'll get a funny blog post out of it.

But sometimes things get serious.

In December of 2012, things were getting serious for me. I was struggling with a sudden recurrence of the panic and anxiety disorder that had crippled me postpartum, and I needed a big fat shovel to dig me out. I looked back through the past year of my life for what had inspired me the most—what had motivated me to keep going even when things were darkest. What came to mind was Drops of Awesome. It was a lesson I'd learned and then shared with several important people in my life. It was something I needed to revisit.

So, I returned to my much-neglected blog, and the post that this book is based on splashed onto the internet. The ripples were small at first. A few friends shared it on Facebook and then a few more. Pretty soon I was hearing from people around the world about how much we had in common and how badly we needed this shift in thinking. When I say "we" needed a shift in thinking, I really mean *we*.

What I learned as hundreds of men and women shared their Drops of Awesome experiences with me was that I am not a special case. I am a thirty-five-year-old mom living in the suburbs outside Seattle, blogging and writing young adult fiction novels. You might be a cattle-ranching bachelor from Texas with a Nutella addiction. I'd be willing to bet our negative inner voices sound nearly identical. I'd also be willing to bet that we're both more awesome than we give ourselves credit for. Why don't we find out?

A SPRINKLE OF REALIZATION

I n high school, I had a friend. At least one. There may have been more. It's hard to remember that far back.

We'll call this friend Lola because I always wanted to have a friend named Lola and now, in print, I do. Lola was delightful in many ways. She had amazing hair and a great laugh. She loved to talk about boys and shoes and all things teenage girl. Most importantly, she was always willing to hang out with me. When I got on the school bus, I always knew my friend would be there, maybe saving me a seat, maybe just waving me over so I wouldn't feel alone.

We spent buckets of time together, and after a while, I started to notice something. With all of her big hair and boy-giggling prowess, she also had a really annoying habit. Lola liked to tell me how lame I was. Pretty much all the time.

"You are such a loser," she'd laugh when I told her about my key chain collection.

"OhMyGoshYou'reSuchaDork!" she'd say, in response to my existence.

Sometimes she didn't say it with words. She'd just give me a sarcastic eye roll to let me know that what I was saying was less than cool—it was ridiculous.

This annoyed me more and more until one day I confronted her about it.

"Lola," I said, "You are always putting me down. I don't like it." I probably said it with much more panache than that, but, like I said, it was a long time ago.

"No I'm not, you loser," she responded without even a hint of irony in her voice. "You're one of my best friends."

You may be asking yourself why I continued hanging out with someone who used verbal abuse as a relationship-building tool and who slowly and systematically chipped away at my self-esteem.

It's a good question—a really good question. What the hay?! I am obviously not a dork, loser, dingbat, waste of space, etc. No one has the right to talk to me like that.

Well, even as an immature and less-than-confident teenager, I figured out that it didn't feel good to be berated all the time, and eventually I stood up for myself to the point that Lola and I were no longer friends. She couldn't or wouldn't change, and when I moved away in the middle of my junior year, we didn't stay in touch.

You may be surprised to learn that, years later, as a grown woman with three children of my own, I made a new friend much like Lola, only far more destructive.

This friend hated to see me succeed. When I laughed, she told me that I didn't deserve to be so happy. When I cried, she told me I had earned every ounce of the heartache I carried. When I served someone, she told me my offering was inadequate. When I screwed up and fell flat on my face, she told me she'd seen my failure coming for a thousand miles.

The worst part is that I kept this friend with me all the time, agreeing with her every harping criticism, and even offering her further evidence to support her claims.

This friend was me—my own inner dialogue.

She lived inside my head and her voice sounded a lot like my voice, only meaner and more jerk-like. I needed to be rid of her, but she'd been part of my entourage for so long, I hardly even noticed her anymore. My destructive negative voice was simply a part of who I was.

Then one morning I had a moment of clarity.

I was walking my son, Oscar, to the bus stop. I didn't often walk him to the school bus. He was in second grade and pretty independent, and I was usually busy getting myself and his sisters ready because I'm semi-nocturnal and I sleep later than I plan to most mornings.

When it was time for school, he would usually say goodbye and head up the hill by himself. But this morning I'd made time, and we were walking together, just the two of us.

About halfway to the bus, Oscar reached out and grabbed my hand in an uninhibited way that I knew wouldn't last forever. He was seven at the time, but unfortunately for me and my wish to freeze all my kids at their current ages, he'd likely keep growing. He'd turn eight and then nine and probably ten after that. How many twelve-year-old boys do you see interdigitating with their mommies? Exactly.

So I squeezed his hand, felt the rare Seattle sun on my face, and told him I loved him. In that moment I was nearly perfectly happy.

Nearly.

Then the thought came into my mind, a gift from that joy-shriveling jerk in my head, *That's awesome that you're walking him to the bus stop and putting on this "mother of the year" act today. What about yesterday and the day before that? You hardly ever walk him to the bus. He's probably holding your hand because he's desperate for the love and attention you haven't been showing him.*

My bubble burst. I looked down into his smiling face.

I am a crap mom, I thought.

But then an alarm went off inside my head, and another thought came.

Kathryn. What is wrong with you? You are being an awesome mom in this moment. Your child is happy. You are loving him and caring for him. He's well fed and dressed. You're walking to the bus stop in the early morning, and you're already wearing a bra, for heck's sake. Do not rob yourself of this moment's joy because of what you failed to do yesterday or what you fear you might not do tomorrow.

This started me thinking of all the times I'd done something good while beating myself up for all the times I hadn't been perfect. My inner voice was suddenly exposed for the destructive harpy that she was. Why had I been listening to her taunts?

You're volunteering at the school? Woopty freakin' doo! You know you picked the easiest assignment this year because you're too concerned with your own personal projects to spend time helping your kids.

Wow. So you cleaned the kitchen today. Want a cookie? That dirty rag has been on the counter for a week and those dishes you so righteously cleaned are from breakfast three days ago. You are embarrassing.

That was really nice of you to offer to babysit while your neighbor had surgery. Remember last week when you knew your friend was depressed and you walked right by with a wave because you didn't want to get sucked into the drama? You don't really care about people. Not all the time.

How harmful are these kinds of thoughts?

As I said goodbye to Oscar and began my walk back home, my mind started to shift. My life could not go on like this. There had to be a way to enjoy these moments, to simply be happy without beating myself up for all my failures. My imperfections weren't going anywhere, but the internal flogging had to stop. I needed to send my negative voice packing and replace it with something, and fast, before it took over completely.

That's when it hit me: *Drops of Awesome!* Every time you do something good, something kind, something productive, it's a Drop in your Bucket of Awesome. You don't lose Drops for every misstep. You can only build. You can only fill.

I walked Oscar to the bus. Bam! Drop of Awesome!

I fed him fruit with breakfast. Drop of Awesome!

I told him I loved him. Drop of Awesome!

I wore a bra and brushed my teeth before schlepping it up that hill. *Two fat Drops of Awesome!*

All day long I chanted these words in my head. I picked up that Tootsie Roll wrapper off the front porch instead of stepping over it for the eleventy hundredth time. Drop of Awesome! I unloaded one dish from the dishwasher when I walked through the kitchen on my way to the bathroom. Drop of Awesome! I texted my sad neighbor to say I was thinking about her. Drop of Awesome! I had an unproductive, critical thought about one of my kids, but I brushed it away and replaced it with love. Drop of Awesome!

When I started thinking about my life in terms of adding these little Drops of Awesome for every tiny act of good, I found that I was doing more and more of them because it's a lot more fun to do good when you're rewarded with joy, rather than being punished with guilt for every failure in your past.

By the end of the day, I realized something important. If I was spending time with my kids, really listening to them with attention, then *I was a good listener*, regardless of the fifty other times I'd brushed them off or multi-tasked while they were talking over the past week. And it felt really good to be that person.

If I was wiping the table after dinner, then I was a person who cleans as she goes.

If I paid today's bills as they came in rather than stashing them on the kitchen's Counter of Doom with all the others, then I was a non-procrastinator, whether or not the Counter of Doom remained.

As I added up these Drops of Awesome, I found that in those moments, I actually became the person I had always wanted to be.

Sometimes I'm afraid to be all the way nice to myself, afraid that I'll be so nice that I give myself permission to spiral downward into slobbering, waste-of-space Kathryn who gets her only Drops of Awesome for such heroic acts as breathing and making nachos. (Don't knock the nachos. I'm pretty sure the FDA counts corn chips and salsa as vegetables for the purpose of school lunch preparation, bless their hearts.)

I think it needs to be said that I've had days where Drops of Awesome for breathing and making and keeping down nachos were heroic accomplishments. There was a day one week when I needed to cry all day. I needed to. I would get up long enough to make a meal, smile at my kids, and press play on Netflix. Then I would curl back up in a ball on my bed with a flannel blankie and sob.

At one point during the day, I started to feel horrible about myself. *You're such a loser. You know better than this. Get off your butt and do something. Lying here is not helping anybody. Your tears are Drops of Failure. So you're having a hard time? You're only making it worse.*

Then I took a second to evaluate. I was going through a family crisis.

And I had been really strong for a really long time. I had comforted everyone else while they cried, and there was no one to comfort me. In that moment, that day, those tears were Drops of Awesome because I was taking time to care for myself—stopping and recognizing that I had feelings too and that my feelings mattered. I wasn't giving up; I was amping up. The trial wasn't going anywhere, and I would be facing it the next day and the next week and the next month. And I had to be strong. So, for one day, being tender with myself was what I needed.

The next day, I got up off the bed and got back to work, not at full-speed Super Kathryn levels, but better than the day before. And the next day was better than that day. If I had continued to beat myself up, rather than letting myself cry and be human and do the best I could at that moment, the healing process would have been much messier.

I reached out to a couple of friends during that time, people who knew, loved, and understood me, people who had the power to help lift me from the darkness.

Do you have any friends like that? On the lines below, write the names of the three most influential people in your life, the people most capable of affecting your mood, motivation, and self-image, for better or for not-so-better.

_____

_____

_____

Think about how they affect you—through words, actions, and even the way you perceive they feel about you. Then take a moment to realize that there is one person who blows them all out of the water in terms of actual influence on your mood and behavior.

That person is you.

If you don't choose to be positive about yourself and your efforts, nothing they say or do can change your mood or self-image. If you are not kind to the one person you have the most influence over in this universe, you will never be ultimately happy, no matter how kind you are to everyone else around you.

Think about that power for a second. No matter what people say about you, there is a gatekeeper who decides which messages get through.

Your best friend says, "You look amazing in that swimsuit!"

You think, *Yeah, for a fat girl.*

The principal congratulates you, "You have done so much to help this school!"

You think, *If only I could give as selflessly as Meg. My impact has actually been pretty meager.*

Your husband complains, "I hate my job."

You think, *He took this job because I asked him to. I am such a nag. If it weren't for me, he'd be happy.*

Those were examples of the you who doesn't allow you to shine—the insecure you, the you who is afraid. If you choose love over fear and decide to be your own personal defender of happiness and joy, the people in your life will not have the power to dictate how you feel about yourself.

I prefer these responses:

The alto next to you jokes, "Why did you even join choir? You are so tone deaf."

You think, *Oh, how I love to sit in the middle of this group of amazing singers. I get better every time I come here. Music just lights me up.*

Your brother says, "Thank you for the birthday call. I haven't heard from you in so long, I thought you'd forgotten about me."

You think, *I'm so glad I reached out to him today. I had no idea he was feeling lonely. This was a great choice.*

Your husband complains, "I hate my job."

You think, *I feel sad for him. I love my day-to-day work, so I have more positivity to give. I'll try to be extra supportive while he's going through this hard time.*

If you've ever heard that negative voice putting you down, and if these ideas resonate with you, then two things are certain: you are someone who cares and you are someone who's trying. If you didn't care about doing right or improving your life, you wouldn't be bothered at all by your perceived failures. I say "perceived" failures because I am certain that who you think you are is far from accurate. When you realize how good you are, it will serve as a springboard to propel you even higher. My hope is that as you notice the tiny Drops of Awesome in your life and focus on the good, you will finally become who you were meant to be and feel giddy doing it.

It's a little silly how pleased I am with myself when I'm collecting and planning Drops of Awesome. Who knew it would feel so good to shine a bathroom faucet after I washed my hands, type two sentences in my latest fiction project when I told myself I had no time to write that day, or Facebook message a friend who's been on my mind for weeks? It only feels good when I let myself feel like I am enough and when I take the time to micro-celebrate. Bam! Drops of Awesome!

What would it hurt to eat one more piece of broccoli, to park one stall farther away at the grocery store for ten more steps of exercise, or to say one more kind thing?

Drops of Awesome is really about allowing yourself to feel joy and to be proud of your small victories. This builds momentum and makes you want more Drops in your bucket. Because of the positive feedback you experience, you are willing to do more, and each tiny step brings you closer to achieving your goals!

When we do not celebrate our small victories, the opposite occurs. Our joy turns to dissatisfaction, our momentum to stagnation, and our direction becomes muddled. We ask questions like, "What's the point? Nothing I do matters anyway. Why don't I just play Plants vs. Zombies for a couple of hours or for the rest of my life?" When we don't let our inner Drops of Awesome collector take over, we're letting that negative voice have free reign to convince us to give up.

What could be more harmful than convincing people that they are worthless, that their good actions will never be good enough, or that it doesn't matter how good they are because there's always something they're not doing and that *one* thing they're not doing is the *only* thing that matters? If you can't stop people from doing good, the next best thing is to make them feel bad about doing good. When you feel bad about making progress, you stop progressing.

You are making better progress than you realize. Take a second and realize it, just a bit. One Drop's worth. What Drops of Progress have you made today?

Do you find yourself more or less likely to reliably make good choices when you focus on your good actions, celebrate the positive, and accept how wonderful your current offering is? More likely. A zillion times more. Consistently working to achieve your goals means never giving up. It means trying. And trying means maintaining the will to try, the belief that you are capable of great things, which begins with the realization that you have accomplished good things . . . today. Drops of Awesome!

Drops of Awesome is not a principle of slacking off or giving yourself permission to be somehow less. It's a principle of giving yourself permission to live fully and to celebrate who you really are. It is a principle of giving yourself permission to be wonderful. Every great effort begins with one small Drop.

Drops of Awesome is powerful because it's a principle of action. You're not sitting on your butt wishing you were better. You *are* better . . . a bit and then a bit more.

This is why I refer to it as my great experiment, possibly the most important experiment of my life. Try it. Experiment with being Awesome. You might surprise yourself with how much change you can effect, one tiny Drop at a time.

What would it feel like to pull ten weeds out of your front walk today, maybe not every day, but just today? How would your life change if you wrote a letter to your grandpa, without dwelling on the fact that you haven't written in far too long or promising yourself that you will write him a letter every week for the rest of his life? Would the feeling in your home change if you said one positive thing to your spouse or sibling the moment you saw his or her face this morning? *This* morning. Right now. Would just that one Drop really change your home? You'll never know unless you perform the experiment.

I magine you're a parent and you have one child who frequently makes you doubt your parenting abilities, your sanity, and your ability to wake up the next morning and Love and Logic® her into submission.

When she sees her little brother, she makes a face specifically designed to cause him soul-crushing anguish. If, by chance, it doesn't work, she just kicks him. When this little girl wants something, she takes it. When she can't take it, she screams for it. She's the flailing psychobot in the Target checkout line, the grimacing ingrate at the extended family Thanksgiving dinner.

You love her and look back on her baby years with longing.

You've done everything you can to help her change. You've shown her love, enlisted the help of her teachers and your parents, offered incentives for good behavior, spoken to her sternly, removed every single item from her room but the nails in the walls, desperately trying to figure out her currency. Then you've tried love again. Nothing is working.

Then one day she wakes up with a sleepy smile on her face. She hugs you good morning and shuffles to the breakfast table where she eats some cereal and then clears her place, putting the milk back in the *actual fridge*. When she passes her brother on the way to the play room, she grunts and nods and when he follows her, she lets him play with her for several minutes peacefully. You watch in amazement and then you react.

How do you react?

"Nice job, Gertrude," you say sarcastically, clapping slowly and deliberately. "You managed to play with Tommy for five minutes without making him cry. Let's see how long that lasts. Oh, and I see you put the milk back in the fridge? What do you want, a medal? I can't count the number of times I've had to clean up after you. You're definitely acting differently this morning. Is this just a fluke or are you trying to trick me into buying you something?"

Are you kidding me?! No! You would rejoice. *Ahhh!* Angels would sing in your head, and you would want to pick that kid up in a huge embrace and twirl around the room with her.

"Gertrude! You are amazing. I love you! Thank you so much for making an effort today. You are showing me who you truly are and that person is a rock star. I'm so proud of you."

Why would you react this way? Because you love her. Because you want her to succeed. She is taking steps in the right direction.

If we never take the little steps in the right direction, we will never get there. Where's there? It's the next Drop closer to being who we desire most to become, who we are destined to be. And if taking steps in the right direction earns us derision and sarcasm, then the steps will stop. We will be paralyzed by our own inadequacies, imagining them to be increasingly larger than they actually are until they fill our whole world and we are frozen in place by our own negative voice. What a waste of life!

Think back to Gertrude. There is nothing a verbal flogging will do to help that child that pure love and encouragement will not do better. Good results are accomplished by nurturing, not nagging. Every time.

So, you're that child. And your inner voice is her parent. How will you treat her in this moment and in the next? Will you value her sincere efforts or will you denigrate her for her childlike mistakes? Will you let her be brilliant or keep her trapped in a prison of shame and loathing?

I have spent time trapped in a cycle where I became obsessed with an ideal that I eventually became convinced I could never reach. Every failure was evidence of my inadequacy and every little success was proof of how far I still had to go.

I lost hope and stopped believing in myself. But how I felt had almost nothing to do with who I actually was and nearly everything to do with what I was telling myself about who I was, what evidence I was collecting.

When I shifted my focus to collecting evidence of my own worth and potential—to actively seeking and capturing my Drops of Awesome—I was motivated and spurred on to greater growth, change, and inspired action. This journal is your new bucket, and in it you will record evidence of your positive influence on the world. You will be capturing motivation.

USING THIS BUCKET

I f there'd been a practical way to write the text of this book on the outside of a bucket and equip you with a dropper that would fill it with words outlining all of your great and small successes and adventures, that would have been ideal. But since I went with a publisher incapable of performing magical enchantments, you're left with this book as a bucket and a pen as a dropper, probably a pen you bought yourself or had to dig out of that one drawer in your kitchen. You know the one.

Regardless, you are ready, armed with all the two tools you need to conduct this great experiment of Awesome. This book is your bucket. It's the paper manifestation of all the efforts you're making. It's evidence of the power of you.

First thing, please skip forward to the journal portion of the book and write the following three Drops of Awesome, and then come back because I've got a few more things to tell you.

1. Purchased this book or accepted it as a gift.
2. Read or skimmed some of the words in said book.
3. Found a pen that contained actual ink.

You're back? Welcome and thanks for doing that. Did you see how easy that was? OK. Those three were extra easy because I already thought of them for you. You are so welcome. But, being *willing* to skip ahead to write down those three things? Drop of Awesome!

Now I will tell you what this book is not. It is not a flotation device and should not be used as such. It is also not a massive to-do list or a chasm of impossible dreams. Do not use it to record things you wish you were doing or Drops of Awesome you intend to collect later . . . sometime . . . because you feel so motivated right now. Just. Don't.

This book will help you become who you are meant to be, but only if you focus on who you are right now and only if you place that focus on the positive. Write down the feats both teensy and gigantic that you are performing to improve your world. These can be in the areas of self-care, home maintenance, education, service, relationships, break dancing, and personal hygiene, whatever makes being you more Awesome.

Here are a few examples from my list:

- cleaned one spot from the carpet while my computer was installing updates
- called my mom to ask about her day
- filled out a field trip form
- began a draft of the work email I've been dreading

- picked up the sock that's been on the floor in the bathroom for six years
- waved at a friend as she was passing
- liked something on Facebook
- answered my daughter's persistent questions even though I was trying to concentrate on typing one complete sentence for this book
- searched for change in my car when I saw a man with a sign on the side of the road asking for help but the light changed before I could give it to him
- let two cars in front of me when leaving the baseball game

You have a couple of options here. You can keep the journal with you, writing down each Drop as you complete it. This option works best for me on days when I'm having trouble moving or breathing and thoughts of Awesome are laughable. These days the Drops read something like "exited bed," "washed face," "replaced toilet paper roll," "read a page of a book," "didn't yell at kids while reminding them to pack their own lunches," "told them I loved them," and "unloaded one dish from the dishwasher." Days like this I need to write as I go to prove to myself that I'm alive and moving in any direction at all.

On other days, you might be cranking out the Awesome. If you are on a roll, moving from room to room, picking things up, curing cancer a bit, and painting the world with rainbows and sunshine, don't stop! Let your momentum build and build. Then, in a quiet moment at the end of the day, stop and let all your tiny Drops sink in. Sit and actually feel the good you've accomplished. Close your eyes and experience the joy of being you. Then pull out your journal and record the highlights. Maybe write a few lines about how you feel. These Drops will be bigger and the list won't be complete, but it doesn't have to be. This journal is about celebrating and finding joy, not feeling guilt. Hopefully you end up doing so many inspired and lovely things that you can't possibly remember them all and by then you won't need to.

Date the pages? Don't date the pages? Whatever works for you. Sometimes it's cool to record dates so you can see progress over time. However, if you're traveling down a particularly bumpy road right now, it may be more helpful to see your cumulative effort and not constantly be comparing today with yesterday. This is not a linear journey, after all.

Most of the writing in this journal will be done by you, but I do have a few more things I'd like to tell you, so I'll be interjecting thoughts throughout—things to keep you going, new ideas to think about, stories I want to share. Thank you for sharing this personal journaling experience with me.

You are doing more good than you currently realize.

You are a person of unspeakably great worth.

You are the only one who will ever get the chance to live your life, and you can do it beautifully.

You deserve to be happy and inherently possess the tools to make it happen.

You are overflowing with Drops of Awesome. Capture them. And when your bucket is full, get a bigger bucket.

The experiment starts . . .

YOUR
BUCKET

Capture that

There is more good in the world than we take time to notice. On this page, capture all the Drops of Goodness you see around you. Did someone let you in front of him or her in traffic? Did a woman entertain your toddler in line at the grocery store? Was there a positive post on Facebook today? Noticing the good in others will help you recognize the good in **yourself.**

goodness!

SO MANY DAYS

I have gone to bed thinking, *I did nothing today*. Really? Do you think it's possible that a day of my life went by where my positive impact on the world was non-existent? How about you? Have you really had a day where you accomplished "nothing"?

DEFINE "NOTHING."

On a day where we feel like that, we're gonna have to scour our brains harder for the Drops of Awesome buried between the nothing.

BUT THEY ARE THERE!

Are you honest enough with yourself to find them?

Quiet the negative voices that zap you of your strength, get out your droppers, and prepare to surprise yourself with what you can accomplish and what you've already done.

HOW BIG IS A drop?

I first shared Drops of Awesome with teenage girls. I asked them to share ideas for Drops and they started listing things like "clean our trashed kitchen," "become a straight-A student," and "do all the laundry in my house."

Although these were great ideas of huge Buckets of Awesome they could accomplish, I encouraged them to focus first on the small things—make eye contact with your mom as if she were an actual person, pick up one piece of dirty laundry, don't moan and sigh when your dad asks you to turn in your cell phone before dinner. A Drop is tiny. All the Drops can lead to major feats of Awesome, but we're recording baby steps here.

Sometimes my tiniest Drops are the ones I'm most proud of because they come on days when the price is high to do anything to keep me moving forward. The darker the moment, the brighter those tiny Drops shine. Make sure you gather and cherish every one.

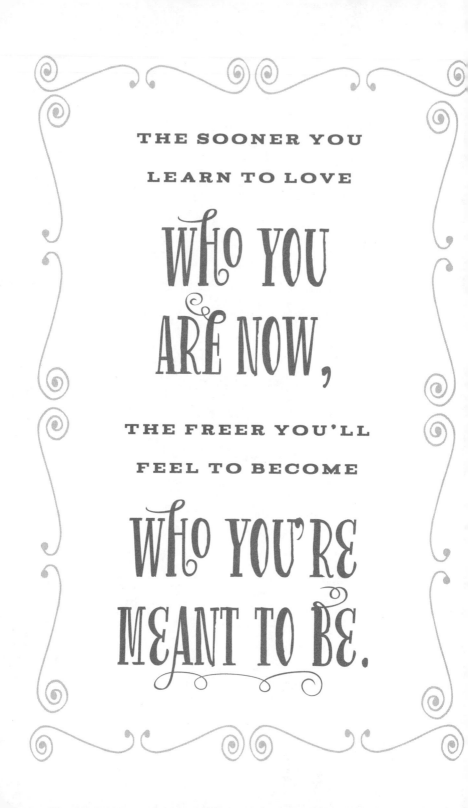

THE SOONER YOU
LEARN TO LOVE
WHO YOU
ARE NOW,
THE FREER YOU'LL
FEEL TO BECOME
WHO YOU'RE
MEANT TO BE.

Next time you walk through the room,

PICK UP THAT WRAPPER INSTEAD OF STEPPING OVER IT.

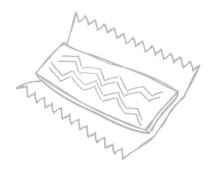

YOU KNOW YOU WANT TO.

HOW MANY TIMES

DID YOU GET

BACK UP TODAY?

YOU CAN'T DO IT ALL.

YOU CAN'T EVEN DO MOST OF IT.

YOU CAN DO Something.

DO IT NOW!

SAY IT OUT LOUD:

"DROP OF AWESOME!"

For one hour, say "Drop of Awesome!" loud and proud every time you have a good thought, do a good deed, or take one action that brings you closer in line with your highest core values.

The past...

is a read-only document with edits turned off. Let it go and focus on

TODAY!

Where we've been doesn't matter nearly as much as where we are now and where, through small acts of power, we are willing to go.

REACH OUT

TO SOMEONE YOU LOVE.

IS HE OR SHE FAR AWAY?

 SEND A TEXT.

 MAIL A HOMEMADE POST CARD.

 LEAVE A VOICE MAIL.

I hate flossing my teeth. Through some sort of magic dentist mind-reading or gum-reading trick, Dr. Hilton always knows whether I've been flossing or not. He's nice about it, suggesting that my visits would be less painful if I'd take the time to floss more thoroughly . . . or at all. Recently he told me that my dental health would improve greatly if each night I would take a minute to reach out and touch the floss. He said I didn't need to use it; I just needed to reach out and touch it. Of course, the point is, that if I'm touching the floss, there's a good chance I'm gonna use it. There's a good chance. But some days? I honestly just reach out and touch the floss.

DROP OF AWESOME.

What lights you up, fills you with joy? Fill yourself with one Drop at a time. Pick a flower and put it in water. Fill yourself and then fill others.

_____
_____
_____
_____
_____
_____
_____
_____
_____
_____
_____
_____
_____
_____
_____
_____
_____
_____
_____
_____
_____
_____
_____
_____

READ A GREAT BOOK.

You don't have to read the whole book.
Just read a chapter. I often don't read
because I tell myself I don't have time
to read the whole thing. What would it
hurt to read one chapter of a great novel,
an uplifting biography, or one quote from
a motivational or religious leader?

WHAT WOULD IT HELP?

When I originally blogged about Drops of Awesome in December of 2012, hundreds of readers wrote to me about their own experiences with that niggling voice telling them they weren't good enough, harassing them most when they were doing their best to make a difference in the world.

One account really stood out to me because I could see myself in her story. Jaune wrote about an experience when she was grabbing some fast food on a chilly day and she noticed a homeless man shivering outside. She decided to buy the man some warm soup. Good story, right? She's such a cool lady. Well, it gets better. By the time she'd finished buying her food, the man had disappeared. Did this stop her from giving her gift of love? No. Jaune circled the block until she found the man, got out of her car, and gave him the steaming cup. As she pulled away, she watched him sit down and happily devour the gift. If the story stopped there, it would be wonderful. Stranger performs random act of kindness. Man is nourished. Everyone wins. But the story didn't end there.

Here's where things started to go south. That selfish wench Jaune had also bought herself some food, and as she took a bite of her own fries, she thought, *A cup of soup? You are so selfish! Why didn't you give him the*

*chicken and the fries? A cup of soup? I'm sure that will
make a big difference in his life. Enjoy your lunch!*

She felt guilty about her warm car and her good food,
and she felt that her offering was small and pathetic.
In short, she felt worse for having served him than she
would have if she'd never noticed his need at all.

That same day she had gotten her kids off to school
in the morning, volunteered at the school for two
hours, participated in a service project to make dinner
for cancer patients' families, made dinner for her own
family, took her kids to their sports activities, helped
them with homework, prayed with them, and tucked
them into bed.

What did she tell me, after recounting all her successes that day? "The things that I focused on? I didn't
buy the homeless man more food—I only made a salad
instead of a main dish for the hospital. We didn't read
scriptures, and of course my house was trashed!" (http://
onceuponafamily-jaune.blogspot.com/2013/01/chicken-
soup-for-my-soul.html)

My eyes filled with tears as I read her story because
it sounded so familiar and at the same time so very
wrong. And Jaune and I are not the only ones who
think this way. Hundreds of men and women shared
their stories in comments and emails after I wrote that

post, stories about how, immediately following moments of inspired action, they found themselves feeling *more* worthless and *less* sure about their ability to ever really accomplish good in their lives.

By thinking of our lives in terms of Drops of Awesome, we focus on the good, the inspiring, even the tiniest spark of progress, and we rejoice in it. How were you awesome today?

CELEBRATE IT.

Sometimes

your best doesn't seem good enough, and sometimes you don't feel good enough to do your best, but you can always do

something.

Chances are, you already have.

WRITE IT DOWN!

What is enough?

When will you be worthy of feeling joy? If not now, when? When will you be blessed enough? Why not now? Are you enough for this moment? Can you let yourself feel like enough?

A delightful friend recently called me.

"I can't stop nagging my husband," she said, "and it's hurting our marriage."

I asked her why she nagged, and she couldn't really pinpoint a reason. I asked her why she didn't just stop, and she said she'd tried so many times to stop that she'd given up hope of ever changing.

"What about today?" I asked. "When he gets home from work today, are you going to nag him?"

There was some hemming and hawing, and she explained that although she didn't intend to nag, it just kind of always happened.

"But today?" I asked again. "When he gets home from work today, are you going to nag him or are you going to plan a different story? You can stop now."

She thought about it for a second, and it hit her like a ton of bricks. *I am not going to nag him today.* She wrote the words **Stop Now** in bold and posted them in her kitchen. And that day, she stopped. She was supportive and loving and not one ounce a nag. She didn't stop nagging all the days forever and ever, but she stopped many of them, and it changed the tone in her home.

What do you wish you could stop doing? OK. Stop today. Stop now.

Low on drops today?

THINK INCENTIVES.

_____
_____
_____
_____
_____
_____

ONE GAME OF BEJEWELED IF YOU
MAIL THOSE TAX DOCUMENTS

_____
_____
_____
_____
_____
_____

A LONG, HOT BUBBLE BATH IF YOU
SCRUB THE BATHROOM

_____
_____
_____
_____
_____
_____

Sometimes success is less about what you do and more about your attitude. I learned this when I potty trained my youngest child. At the beginning, she had accidents a lot. She would stand right next to the potty and just let it rip all over the floor. Then she'd look at me nonchalantly and say, "I just peed in my pants because I really, really wanted to." This drove me batty.

Then one day, something clicked. Ivy discovered that she really *did* want to use the potty. The only problem was, she hadn't figured out exactly *how* to stay dry. She'd hold it as long as possible and then run to the potty, only to lose control inches away from her goal. She would cry in frustration and say, "Mom. I really, really want to be dry next time."

The basic rigmarole was the same. I was still cleaning up urine, but knowing that she was doing her best and that she wanted to do better made it OK somehow. It was all in her attitude and intention.

If you're having a hard time making it, not living up to the expectations you've set for yourself, think about your intentions. Are you trying? Do you have a desire to improve? Those are Drops of Awesome too. Give yourself a break, clean up the mess, and try one more time. You'll get where you want to be eventually, and in the meantime, give yourself credit for your attitude.

SOME-TIMES I ONLY DO A JOB HALFWAY.

THEN I ONLY DO IT HALFWAY AGAIN.

WHAT DO TWO HALVES MAKE?

DROPS OF AWESOME!

PERFECTIONISM

can be crippling when we decide we want
to be perfect now, we want to be perfect
alone, and we want to be perfect in
comparison.

You say you want to do your best, but you
really want to do Sarah's best or your
own best from three years ago when your
health was better. Don't compare your
best with anyone else's, even your own at
another moment in time. Think honestly
about what *you* can do in *this moment*.
Then do that. Drop of Awesome!

CHANGE

YOUR

PERSPECTIVE.

WHAT ARE YOU DOING RIGHT
NOW TO MAKE A DIFFERENCE,
EVEN A TINY ONE?

T here are things I want to do and things I have to do. Sometimes these interests collide, but usually if there's something I have to do, it suddenly falls into the category of things I don't want to do. This doesn't make a whole lot of sense, but I think most of us do this. I have to do it? Yuck. Work.

So we procrastinate. The next time there's something you need to do but you're tempted to do something you want to do instead, try postponing the fun, but only a Drop's worth.

You need to take out the trash, but you really want to watch your favorite show? Say, "I'm going to plop on the couch and watch TV right now, but . . . before I do, there's just one more thing I need to accomplish. I will remove the full trash bag from the can in preparation for my pro-crastinated trash taking out later tonight.

Just do one more thing. Just one. You'll probably find it hard to stop with the trash job half completed. You'll likely just tie it up and take it outside. But, if you don't, the trash is one step closer to its way out the door. Bam! Drop of Awesome.

Imperfection

ISN'T FAILURE.

It's opportunity for growth. The only
failure is wallowing in defeat and
accepting it. Accept who you are now,
a hero on the path of who you will
eventually become.

WRITE A STATEMENT

OF WHO YOU ARE AND WHO YOU DESIRE TO BE. READ IT THROUGH EACH MORNING AS PART OF YOUR WAKE-UP ROUTINE.

Do you ever picture where you want to be in fifty years or what you hope to have accomplished at the end of your life? I think of this as living with a lifetime perspective. When you have a lifetime perspective, you work to make your daily actions match your highest long-term goals.

But sometimes a lifetime perspective blows my mind a little. Sometimes I can barely focus on getting through the day. I find that it helps to ask myself where my perspective is right now and then work to expand it just a bit. Honestly, there are days when I give no forethought whatsoever to my actions. I am living moment by moment, dousing one fire after another and hoping we all make it to bedtime in one piece. On days like that, it helps to think of life in terms of a ten-minute perspective. What can I do right now that will make my life better in ten minutes? What do I want to have accomplished ten minutes from now, and what can I do to forward that goal?

Once I master the ten-minute perspective, I can focus on my goals for the day. What do I realistically want my life to look like by the end of the day? What Drop of Awesome should I do right now to get closer to that ideal?

Then I expand to a one-year plan and then a ten-year. Start where you are and continue to expand your perspective. If you wake up tomorrow and you're back to the one-minute plan, rinse and repeat.

CHOOSE

YOUR INNER DIALOG FOR THE
DAY. CREATE A NEW CHANT.

"I AM STRONG. I AM ORGANIZED.
I KNOW MY PRIORITIES."

WRITE YOUR OWN AND THEN
KEEP IT ON YOUR MIND.

I recently completed my first triathlon with a friend who is much smaller than me. She's shorter up and down *and* side to side. It took me a couple of years to lose enough weight that I felt comfortable competing in a major athletic event and several months of tiny Drops to feel fit enough.

It occurred to me one day as we were training that I had become my own After Picture. I was thinner, fitter, and more confident, and I was a few days away from being a medal-wearing triathlete. Now, I wasn't Stephanie's After Picture. If anything, I was a puffed up version of *her* Before Picture. But it's okay. I'm not Stephanie. I'm me. And today, I am my own After Picture.

I am what comes after all the struggles and learning and growth and improvements of all the years of my life. My After Picture may be the same as your Before Picture, but that's OK. I love me. One day, who I am today will become my Before Picture too.

TALK TO
YOURSELF
THE WAY
YOU'D TALK
TO YOUR

DEAREST

FRIEND.

Did you know I was a model? Well, so are you. Your friends and loved ones look to you as an example. Do you want the people you love most to be as hard on themselves and as unrelenting in their pursuit of perfection as you are? Do you want them to put themselves down and be mired in insecurity and feelings of failure? Be as kind to yourself as you want them to be to themselves.

YOUR BRAIN

IS BROADCASTING A

24-HOUR RADIO SHOW.

How will you fill the air time? What guests will you invite to join you? How will you set the tone for your personal station? What will your theme music sound like?

It's the middle of the night, and I can't sleep because I'm thinking about you. You, the face looking down at this journal, you who might not believe that she is progressing or making a big enough difference in this world.

I have good news and bad news. The bad news is that you are way wrong, and the voices you've been listening to are unreliable, unhelpful, and unproductive. The good news is that you are progressing and you are making a positive difference in the world. I am kept awake tonight by my desire for you to block out the destructive crud that you've been telling yourself for years. Even block out my voice for a minute and listen to your heart.

I'll do it with you. It's been too long since I stopped what I was doing, put my hand on my heart, and really let myself feel who I am. Find a quiet place where you can sit comfortably alone. Laugh a little, busy people. I'll wait. Pick your moment. Maybe it's late tonight or early tomorrow morning.

I'm going to stop writing and you're going to stop reading. Put down the journal, close your eyes, put your hand on your heart, and just breathe. Focus all of your energy on your heart, the feel of it beating, the rise and fall of your chest. Open yourself up to feel any thoughts that come from your core. If it's comfortable, go for what feels like at least five minutes. Then meet me back here. Ready . . . go.

You're back.

What did you feel? Nothing? Try it again tomorrow. Something negative? Write it down and then write down a true contradictory response. If the thought came, "You're terrible at your job," write, "I am amazing at my job." Or if you really don't believe that, try "I work hard at my job. I can improve every day." Then try the exercise again with a clear mind and see if you feel something different.

Did you feel something good? Warmth, tears, recognition that at a heart level you have worth, that you are making better progress than you realized, that you are worth loving, honoring, and being valued? If you felt any of these things, please write them down in this journal. A lightness, a hope, a joy, a comfort, a peace, or a glimmer of calm that was buried so deep you'd lost hope it was there? Write it down.

When I do this exercise, I often feel love—for myself, for others, and for the life I have the chance to live. And love fuels me. It opens my eyes to truth and possibility.

Choose to be happy by choosing to do more of the things that will make you ultimately happy.

Choose to be happy by feeling the power of those choices, by celebrating *you*!

THE PEOPLE

YOU WANT TO

BE WITH ARE

THOSE THAT

MAKE YOU FEEL

ABOUT

YOURSELF.

My grandma Peg was a delightful person. She loved me and made that love clear with every hug, crocheted blanket, and beautifully penned letter. Most years on my birthday and some other times too, my grandma would send me the most thoughtful letters. They were full of encouragement and memories of when I was young. They were long and written in lovely cursive. I looked forward to the surprise of a letter from Grandma Peg. There was, however, one thing I did not enjoy about her letters. They inevitably began with an apologetic rant about what a terrible grandma she was and how sorry she was for how long it had been since her last letter.

Drops of Awesome, Grandma! Wherever she is right now, I hope she knows how much those letters meant to me, and I hope she's lost the Rotten Grandma Syndrome. Those letters remind me not to waste energy on regrets when I'm currently putting my best foot forward.

Note to my future grandchildren: I will begin every email to you with a rant about how Awesome I am for writing it. Love, Me

Have you ever said any of these things?

"I always fight with my mother. Our relationship is broken."

"I'm kind of a nag."

"I don't really have any friends."

"I gossip and I always end up hurting people I love."

"I can't stop spending money. I will never get out of debt."

"My yard is always a disaster."

These things are lies, depending on the next decision you make, the next Drop of Awesome you put in your bucket. You may have done these things in the past, but they don't define you. You can change this very instant. You may not think you can change permanently, but you can change the next choice you make. And, as you change that one next tiny choice, you may think, *I got this one Drop of Awesome but I may never be able to get another one again.*

And that's OK.

You made the right choice once. And in that moment you were the person you wanted to be, and that was a triumph. Maybe for one night, you were a person who went to bed early. Then one morning you woke up and the first words out of your mouth were positive so you were a morning person in that moment. Bam! Drop of Awesome.

You do not need to wait three months to be who you want to be. Pick up ten things right now and say, "Drops of Awesome! I am someone who takes care of my house. That is who I am. I have proof."

Think about it this way. If you get up early one morning and go running, in that moment, you are one of those early morning running people. Those people are amazing. Maybe, though, after doing it once, your body and mind rebel and you can never get yourself up again at 5:00 a.m. to run like a freezing madwoman in the dark. Does the current lack of running erase that one day when you were an early morning running person? Nope. Your body is one run healthier. Your story is one Drop more full of Awesome. At the very least, you can always look back and think, *Remember when I was a runner? That was so self-controlled and health-conscious of me. I am never doing that again. What Drop of Awesome can I do next?*

Usually when I start focusing on resolutions or trying to be better, I get scared. What if I can't do this forever? What if I say I'm going to be Awesome and then I'm not? What I love about a Drops of Awesome approach is that there are no strings attached to each act of good you do. Doing it once won't lock you in for life or label you a failure if you can't keep it up forever.

If I say, "I want to go to bed early tonight and be an early-to-bedder," that does not mean that if tomorrow I stay up a little late, I'm a failure. What it means is I made an awesome choice one night. I might do it again. But I also have the option of doing this one Drop and then walking away, one improvement just to see how it feels.

Who do you want to be when you grow up?

Take a minute to think about one person you really look up to. To get where she is, I'm sure she had to go through a process of becoming. Picture what Drops she must have plunked into her bucket when she was at your stage to prepare her to become who she is today. Choose one of those Drops and do it now. Bam! How does that feel?

Not all weaknesses are really weaknesses if you look at them from another angle. Write some of your weaknesses and then write about how they are or could become strengths.

EXAMPLES:

I talk too much and sometimes over-share: I put people at ease and make them laugh.

I can't stop eating: I love and appreciate great food. I could learn to cook some amazing, healthy dishes for me and my family to indulge in.

NOW YOU GO:

_____
_____
_____
_____
_____
_____
_____
_____
_____
_____
_____
_____
_____
_____
_____
_____
_____
_____
_____

M y son has a checklist of things he's supposed to do each day: focus in class, bring home math worksheets, avoid injuring his younger sister, brush teeth, etc. He gets points for each thing he does, and when enough points accrue, he gets a reward.

When we started this process, we sat down the first night for the reckoning, and he bawled over every task he had not accomplished. I pointed out that he'd gotten several points. He countered that he'd missed three. I countered that he was now seven points closer to reaching his reward. He pointed out that he could have been three points closer.

Finally I asked him if he knew about my daily checklist.

"No."

"Do you think I check off every single thing every single day?"

"Yes?"

"Ha. No. Do you think I've ever had a day where I checked off every single item?"

He looked confused so I answered my own question.

"No! I do the best I can, and I count myself as Awesome for every single thing I do. The things I miss will still be there the next day. So I try again."

He smiled. And he got it. He makes progress every day, without the tears. Who needs to cry because he just moved closer to his goal? Nobody.

you feel you need to write things down in a
to-do list, think of it as a

smorgasbord.

Mmmmmmmm.

So many great things to choose from. You
know you can't possibly do them all, or at
least not without making yourself sick, so you
pick the ones that will bring you the most joy
and do those. Give yourself credit for what
you check off, not criticism for what you leave
behind. Tomorrow is another day. You can
return to the smorgasbord then.

Overwhelming to-do list?

WHY NOT WRITE A "DONE LIST" INSTEAD?

T he more you take time to notice your own positive intentions, tiny offerings of goodness, and to celebrate being you, the easier it will become. Hopefully it's almost second nature now. You could be an expert in giving yourself permission to move on from your mistakes and start fresh each minute as you reach for one more Drop of Awesome.

Do you do the same for others? Is there someone in your life who may be hard to love at the moment, someone about whom you only notice the negative? Choose a page for her in this journal and start up a collection, a page full of the best of her, a page full of all the times you notice her trying, succeeding even a little, being even a tiny bit lovable.

You're like a spy, collecting evidence of her worth. The more you write, the more you will value her and the more she will feel your love.

A DOWNPOUR OF PROGRESS

So, I'm collecting all these Drops of Awesome, journaling about how great I am in all my imperfect brilliance. But what about goals and ambitions? How do those fit into this approach?

At some point, you may be ready to record a few of your big dreams. *A few.* Choose a page and write them down. Get out some colored pencils, markers, or crayons, and underline or highlight each goal in a different color. Now go back through the journal and underline or highlight any Drops of Awesome that you can see are leading you toward that goal.

Set goals. Set big goals. Then break them down into tiny Drops and collect them one at a time. The most important thing is to give yourself real credit for any progress you're making and not to beat yourself up when you think you've fallen short. Don't crush your joy by using your goals as an excuse to spiral into a place of guilt, shame, or paralyzing fear. Your goals should propel you to positive action. They can't do that unless you let them.

Think of your goals as an adventure. Think of them as an ideal to strive for. Love and nurture yourself into achieving them, one Drop at a time.

Imagine you're at a party and you decide to eat a fresh chocolate chip cookie. It's warm, moist, and delicious, and you enjoy eating it.

But then you notice someone else at the party eating a dense chocolate brownie with vanilla ice cream on top, smothered in thick hot fudge.

You look around and notice that there's a whole table of treats you hadn't noticed when you'd eaten earlier. It's covered with hot fudge brownies, decadent cheesecake, and a dozen other delectable treats.

Although you're already full, the choices make your mouth water, and you wish you'd known all the options when you chose your dessert.

Does knowing there were other desserts diminish the deliciousness of the cookie you already devoured? No. The experience is in the past and can't change, although your perception of it might.

Could you have chosen a better treat if you'd known about all the options? Maybe.

The truth is, you ate a delicious cookie. Your tummy is one cookie happier.

Sometimes in life I do nothing because there's so much to do and I worry that I'll pick the wrong thing. But as long as I choose to do something good, get one more Drop of Awesome, my bucket will be one Drop fuller. I might not always choose the best or the biggest Drop. I might not even know until later about all the Drops I could have had at any given time, but as long as I keep doing something, I continue to progress.

Progress is not always linear. Each step back in the right direction moves you closer to where you want to be.

Are you making progress?

Hopefully, you are. If you're not, you may want to start thinking of ways you can incorporate more Drops of Nurturing or Drops of Nuclear Scientistry or whatever else you want to achieve into your daily routines. Think about it, but do not stress.

Then, on your goal page and your goal page only, write down a few ideas of Drops you'd like to get sometime, to keep them fresh in your mind. If you tackle one of them, great! If not, write down what you *did* accomplish.

One thing you've accomplished is making it to the end of this book! Maybe it's full to the brim with your Awesome and you're ready for a bigger bucket. Perhaps you're one of those skip-to-the end kinds of people, and now you're planning to go back and start the real journey. It's possible you simply read my words and you're ready to move on with your life. I hope you wrote something or at least doodled in the margins a little.

Whatever process brought you to this page, I hope it's becoming second nature for you to focus on the good in yourself and others. I hope you have a deeper appreciation for all you accomplish in the world and a greater desire to do more, one tiny Drop at a time. You may be achieving so much that you've become more strategic in your Drops, carefully planning all the amazing ripples you'll generate daily.

Whether you're in the market for more Awesome real estate because this bucket is full or whether you're just getting started with the experiment, know that the journey is not over. It will never be over. There will be days when you forget that each step you take in the right direction leads you closer to your goals. There might even be times when you completely lose sight of how incredibly important your every effort is to the world. When this happens, picture a dropper in your hand and imagine squeezing out just one Drop of the best you can offer in that moment.

You've got this. Go forth. Be Awesome.

Acknowledgments

This book could never have happened without everyone who embraced Drops of Awesome when I first posted it on DaringYoungMom.com. Thank you for sharing your stories with me. You are inspiring.

Thanks to Dan, my best friend and biggest source of Awesome, and to Heather, Jenny, Katie, Linda, KayLynn, and all the others who read early drafts and offered valuable feedback. Thank you, Andrea, for letting me share this with the girls.

I appreciate Christopher, David, Aimee, and everyone at Familius for envisioning this book, guiding me through the process, and blowing my mind with your gorgeous design and wonderful insight.

Finally, thank you to Claire, Oscar, and Ivy for being magical children and fabulous friends. My gratitude goes out to you and all of my endlessly supportive family.

About Kathryn Thompson

Kathryn Thompson lives in the Seattle suburbs with her computer genius husband and three young kids. She is addicted to words and wants to borrow your kayak if you're not using it this weekend. You can follow her adventures at DaringYoungMom.com.

About Familius

Welcome to a place where mothers are celebrated, not compared. Where heart is at the center of our families, and family at the center of our homes. Where boo-boos are still kissed, cake beaters are still licked, and mistakes are still okay. Welcome to a place where books—and family—are beautiful. Familius: a book publisher dedicated to helping families be happy.

VISIT OUR WEBSITE: WWW.FAMILIUS.COM

Our website is a different kind of place. Get inspired, read articles, discover books, watch videos, connect with our family experts, download books and apps and audiobooks, and along the way, discover how values and happy family life go together.

JOIN OUR FAMILY

There are lots of ways to connect with us! Subscribe to our newsletters at www.familius.com to receive uplifting daily inspiration, essays from our Pater Familius, a free ebook every month, and the first word on special discounts and Familius news.

BECOME AN EXPERT

Familius authors and other established writers interested in helping families be happy are invited to join our family and contribute online content. If you have something important to say on the family, join our expert community by applying at:
www.familius.com/apply-to-become-a-familius-expert

GET BULK DISCOUNTS

If you feel a few friends and family might benefit from what you've read, let us know and we'll be happy to provide you with quantity discounts. Simply email us at specialorders@familius.com.

Website: www.familius.com
Facebook: www.facebook.com/paterfamilius
Twitter: @familiustalk, @paterfamilius1
Pinterest: www.pinterest.com/familius

The most important work you ever do will be within the walls of your own home.